BRITANNICA

LEARNING LIBRARY

Remarkable People in History

Learn about famous lives from different times and places

ENCYCLOPÆDIA

Britannica®

CHICAGO   LONDON   NEW DELHI   PARIS   SEOUL   SYDNEY   TAIPEI   TOKYO

This book is to be returned on or before
the last date stamped below

Schools

Remarkable People in History

INTRODUCTION

Who is known as the Father of Europe? What did Tenzing Norgay climb? How did Cleopatra die? Why did Gandhi march to the sea?

In *Remarkable People in History,* you'll discover answers to these questions and many more. Through pictures, articles, and fun facts, you'll learn about extraordinary people who have changed the course of history.

To help you on your journey, we've provided the following signposts in *Remarkable People in History*:

■ **Subject Tabs**—The coloured box in the upper corner of each right-hand page will quickly tell you the article subject.

■ **Search Lights**—Try these mini-quizzes before and after you read the article and see how much - *and how quickly* - you can learn. You can even make this a game with a reading partner. (Answers are upside down at the bottom of one of the pages.)

■ **Did You Know?**—Check out these fun facts about the article subject. With these surprising 'factoids', you can entertain your friends, impress your teachers, and amaze your parents.

■ **Picture Captions**—Read the captions that go with the photos. They provide useful information about the article subject.

■ **Vocabulary**—New or difficult words are in **bold type**. You'll find them explained in the Glossary at the end of the book.

■ **Learn More!**—Follow these pointers to related articles in the book. These articles are listed in the Table of Contents and appear on the Subject Tabs.

Britannica
LEARNING LIBRARY

Have a great trip!

Cathy Freeman was the first Aboriginal to win an individual medal in an Olympic event. She won the 400-metre race at the 2000 Olympics in Sydney, Australia.

© Duomo/Corbis

Remarkable People in History

TABLE OF CONTENTS

The Emperor
and the Right Way of Living

Some 2,200 years ago the emperor Ashoka ruled India. Like many ancient rulers, he expanded his empire by conquering new lands. But unlike most rulers, Ashoka suddenly turned his back on warfare and began to govern according to the non-violent beliefs of Buddhism.

It is said that Ashoka became a Buddhist when he saw the horrors caused by the wars he'd led. After that, he decided to serve his subjects and all humanity instead of conquering others. He called this 'conquest by *dharma*'. In India *dharma* means the 'right way of living' and 'universal truth'. This includes being honest, truthful, and kind. It also means being merciful, generous, and thoughtful.

The emperor himself would often tour the countryside, preaching his belief in *dharma* to the people. Ashoka also appointed '*dharma* ministers' to help relieve people's sufferings. These ministers were assigned to look after the special needs of women and people living in religious communities.

Ashoka passed laws to prevent cruelty to animals and had hospitals built for both people and animals. He also started construction projects to make all people's lives easier. Trees were planted on roadsides, wells were dug, and watering sheds and rest houses were built.

The only recognition Ashoka wanted was for people to remember that he had ruled according to *dharma*. To preserve his ideas, Ashoka had his teachings carved on rocks and pillars (columns) in public areas. These inscriptions are called the Rock **Edicts** and Pillar Edicts. The most famous is the lion pillar found at Sarnath, which has become India's national emblem.

SEARCH LIGHT

Ashoka was an Indian
a) mathematician.
b) emperor.
c) priest.

LEARN MORE! READ THESE ARTICLES…
JULIUS CAESAR • CHARLEMAGNE
MAHATMA GANDHI

DID YOU KNOW?
Despite his reputation as a kind and generous ruler, some stories describe Ashoka as cruel and ruthless. According to one story, he had all his brothers killed in order to seize the throne.

Sarnath, an archaeological site in northern India, is said to be the place where the Buddha first preached to his followers. Ashoka built this *stupa* (shrine) and others, as well as pillars, to honour the event.
© Brian A. Vikander/Corbis

Rome's Remarkable General and Statesman

Julius Caesar was a brilliant general and a gifted writer. But most important, he helped create the ancient Roman Empire.

Early in his career Caesar formed a **bond** with the two most powerful men in Rome - the wealthy Crassus and the general Pompey. In 59 BC they helped elect Caesar as one of Rome's two consuls, the government's highest rank. After a year as consul, Caesar left Rome to govern Gaul (now France). There he earned a reputation as a military leader. He stopped uprisings and invasions, and he even landed in Britain. Caesar also wrote detailed accounts of his battles.

Sculpture of Julius Caesar, in the National Museum in Naples.
© Bettmann/Corbis

While Caesar was in Gaul, Crassus was killed. Pompey now controlled Rome and he turned against Caesar. He declared Caesar a criminal and ordered him to break up his army. Instead, Caesar declared war and marched to Rome. Pompey fled to Greece.

At that time Rome was governed by a senate (a supreme council). But Caesar felt the government was corrupt and needed a strong leader. In 49 BC he declared himself **dictator**, and he spent five years fighting a civil war against Pompey to make his rule secure. Some of the Roman senators worried that Caesar had too much power. On 15 March 44 BC they murdered Caesar on the floor of the Senate.

In the short time he led Rome, Caesar proved to be a great statesman. The changes he made helped begin the 500-year Roman Empire. And for almost 2,000 years after his death, some world leaders used a form of the title 'caesar' (such as 'Kaiser' in Germany and 'czar' in Russia).

LEARN MORE! READ THESE ARTICLES...
ASHOKA • CHARLEMAGNE • CLEOPATRA

By crossing over the stream known as the Rubicon in 49 BC, Caesar basically declared war against the Roman senate. 'Crossing the Rubicon', the subject of this engraving, became a phrase that means taking a step from which there's no turning back.
© Bettmann/Corbis

SEARCH LIGHT

Fill in the gap: Caesar took power in Rome after defeating _____, his former political supporter.

Answer: Caesar took power in Rome after defeating Pompey, his former political supporter.

9

DID YOU KNOW?
Castro was a very good baseball player. It is said he once even tried out for the Senators, a professional baseball team in Washington, D.C.

The Man Who Changed Cuba

In the 1950s General Fulgencio Batista ruled the Caribbean island of Cuba. His rule was harsh and often violent, and some large American companies grew rich while many Cubans remained poor. Fidel Castro was a young lawyer who believed Batista's rule was unfair. There were no free elections in Cuba, so Castro organized a military force to overthrow Batista.

Castro bought guns with his own money and attacked Batista's forces in 1953. The attack failed badly, and after two years in prison Castro went to Mexico to make a new plan. Soon he and about 80 other **rebels** arrived in Cuba. They hid in the mountains and fought a **guerrilla** war using small-scale battles and making hit-and-run attacks. Batista finally fled Cuba in 1959.

> True or false? The United States has supported Castro's rule in Cuba.

Castro became Cuba's leader and created a **communist** government to

Fidel Castro in 1960.
© Bettmann/Corbis

control all parts of Cuba's life. After a while, the people lost many of the same rights that Batista had taken away, and Cuban businesses did not create new wealth. Many Cubans left their homeland or tried to do so. But Castro also greatly increased many benefits to the Cuban people. Education and health services were free, and every citizen was guaranteed work.

The United States, Cuba's near neighbour, strongly opposed Castro's government. They even tried to overthrow it in 1961. And in 1962 Cuba was at the centre of a dangerous clash between the United States and the **Soviet Union**. Castro had let Soviet **nuclear weapons** be set up in Cuba.

Today Cuba is one of the last communist countries in the world. In the late 20th century there was unrest among Cubans, and Castro relaxed some of his strictest controls. Still, after more than 40 years, he remains Cuba's powerful leader.

LEARN MORE! READ THESE ARTICLES...
SIMÓN BOLÍVAR • NELSON MANDELA • MAO ZEDONG

**Fidel Castro still speaks out strongly against people
who disagree with his communist government in Cuba.
Here he speaks at a rally in 2003.**
© AFP/Corbis

Answer: FALSE. Since the early 1960s, the United States has opposed Castro and has supported attempts to overthrow him.

Dis ist der gstalt und biltnus glåch

kaiser Karlus der das Remisch reich den tettschen undern trüng undern macht

kazolius impaint   magnus Annis.14 2

Charlemagne's empire survived for only a brief time after he died. But no other ruler in the European Middle Ages had such a deep and long-lasting effect.
© Ali Meyer/Corbis

The Father of Europe

During the Middle Ages (about AD 500-1500) one of the most powerful European kings was Charlemagne. Charlemagne was a Frank. The Franks were a people who lived in parts of modern France and Germany. When he became the one and only ruler of the Frankish lands in AD 771, Charlemagne wanted to make his kingdom bigger and stronger. He also wanted to spread Christianity and protect the Roman Catholic church.

Which of these did Charlemagne **not** build?
a) pyramids
b) schools
c) libraries

With this plan in mind, Charlemagne spent 30 years battling the Saxons, another Germanic people. In these and many other wars, Charlemagne gained control over much of western Europe, including what is now France, Switzerland, Belgium, the Netherlands, and half of Italy and Germany.

In the year 800, the **pope** crowned Charlemagne the emperor of the Romans. This made him the first of many emperors who would rule until

Illuminated (richly decorated) manuscript showing Charlemagne meeting Pope Adrian I.
© Archivo Iconografico, S.A./Corbis

1806. Charlemagne reorganized the government in his empire. He worked with leaders of the church to improve the church and government. And he sent out special agents to ensure that his laws were being obeyed.

Charlemagne brought about many improvements in the kingdom. He set up a new money system and reformed the law courts. He built a large court library and set up a school at his palace court. He was concerned with educating the ordinary people and improving the learning of priests. He hoped education would make his people better Christians.

Charlemagne died in 814. Today he is remembered as one of the most important rulers in European history. In fact, he's sometimes called the father of Europe.

LEARN MORE! READ THESE ARTICLES...
ASHOKA • JULIUS CAESAR • EMPRESS OF CHINA

Answer: a) pyramids

Queen of Egypt

She spoke nine languages, was a good mathematician, and had a great head for business. And she would use both her intelligence and her beauty to hold on to power. Today, Cleopatra VII Thea Philopator of Egypt is still an amazing historical figure.

Cleopatra was the second daughter of King Ptolemy XII. When her father died in 51 BC, 18-year-old Cleopatra was supposed to rule Egypt with her 15-year-old brother, Ptolemy XIII. In a few years, her brother's supporters drove Cleopatra from power. But later the Roman leader Julius Caesar helped her get her throne back. War soon broke out. In 47 BC Cleopatra's brother and co-ruler drowned. By law she couldn't rule alone, so she married her 11-year-old brother.

Cleopatra returned to Rome to live with Caesar and had a son by him named Caesarion. But Caesar was murdered in 44 BC, and Cleopatra lost her strongest supporter. She soon went back to Egypt. With Caesar dead, the two most powerful men in Rome were Octavian and Mark Antony. When Antony wanted to invade Persia, he invited Cleopatra to meet him.

Antony quickly fell in love with Cleopatra and married her. But he was also married to Octavian's sister. An angry Octavian declared war against Antony and eventually defeated him. Antony died in Cleopatra's arms.

Cleopatra did not want to live without Antony. The story is that she had an asp (a kind of snake) brought to her, and when it bit her, Cleopatra died at the age of 39. The Egyptians believed that death by snakebite made you **immortal**. Cleopatra didn't live forever, but her legend has lasted more than 2,000 years.

LEARN MORE! READ THESE ARTICLES…
JULIUS CAESAR • GOLDA MEIR
ANWAR EL-SADAT

SEARCH LIGHT

How many times did Cleopatra rule Egypt?

DID YOU KNOW?
William Shakespeare wrote a play about Egypt's most famous queen, called *Antony and Cleopatra*.

This image of the Egyptian queen Cleopatra appears on a temple of the goddess Hathor in Dandarah, Egypt. Hathor was the goddess of the sky, of women, and of love.
The Art Archive

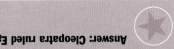
Answer: Cleopatra ruled Egypt twice.

A Clever, Courageous Queen

When Elizabeth I became queen of England, few thought she would last very long. But Elizabeth I not only ruled for almost half a century. She became one of England's greatest rulers.

Elizabeth was the daughter of Anne Boleyn, King Henry VIII's second wife. Henry also had a daughter, Mary, from his first marriage, and had a son, Edward, from his third. After Henry's death, Edward ruled for a short time until he died. Mary ruled for three years before she too died. In 1558 Elizabeth became the queen of England at the age 25.

Oil painting of Elizabeth I with members of her court.
© Stapleton Collection/Corbis

At the time, England was poor, weak, and torn by **conflict** between different groups. The people hoped Elizabeth would marry a strong man who would guide her. But Elizabeth had no desire to share her power. She was determined to be a successful queen, so she gathered experienced and trustworthy advisers. Elizabeth herself had a good education and was very clever and courageous.

The queen encouraged English sailors to travel to distant parts of the world. Captains such as Francis Drake brought back riches and found new trade routes to the Americas, Asia, and Africa. As trade developed with other lands, England grew wealthy. Under Elizabeth, England also experienced a Renaissance, or 'rebirth' of the arts. Some of the famous writers of the period were William Shakespeare, Christopher Marlowe, Francis Bacon, Edmund Spenser, and John Donne.

By the time Elizabeth died in 1603, England had become both rich and strong. The 45 years of her **reign** became known as the Elizabethan Age.

LEARN MORE! READ THESE ARTICLES...
JULIUS CAESAR • CLEOPATRA • GOLDA MEIR

Elizabeth I, popularly known as Good Queen Bess, became queen after the death of her half sister in 1558. She loved showy clothing and jewels.
© Archivo Iconografico, S.A./Corbis

DID YOU KNOW?

During Elizabeth's rule, Spain attacked England with a great fleet of ships called the Spanish Armada. England's victory over the Spanish forces saved the country from becoming part of the Spanish empire.

SEARCH LIGHT

Elizabeth ruled England only after her
a) two sisters ruled.
b) sister and brother ruled.
c) two brothers ruled.

Answer: b) sister and brother ruled.

大清當今慈禧端佑康頤昭豫莊誠壽恭欽獻崇熙聖母皇太后

The Dragon Lady

One of the most powerful women in Chinese history was Cixi. She controlled China for more than 40 years in the late 1800s. Cixi was so **ruthless** and dangerous that some people called her the Dragon Lady.

In Western countries such as Great Britain and the United States, Cixi was also known as the Empress Dowager. But she was never really an empress. She was just the mother of the emperor's only son. When the emperor died, she helped her 6-year-old son, who was heir to the throne, rule China. She still had power when her son was old enough to rule by himself. Then he died, and the Dragon Lady made sure her 4-year-old nephew became the new emperor. This was against the law, but she helped him rule too.

The Dragon Lady lived in a group of palace buildings called the Forbidden City, within the city of Beijing. Only the servants who lived there too ever saw Cixi. She spoke to all her visitors from a large red throne shaped like a dragon that was hidden behind a silk screen. Every one of her orders ended with the warning 'Hear and obey'.

Under Cixi the Chinese government became very dishonest. Many believed that Cixi had had many people murdered. In 1908, when the Dragon Lady was dying, she had her nephew, the emperor, poisoned. She wanted to make sure that he died first and thus would never rule without her.

SEARCH LIGHT

Did anybody ever see the Empress of China?

DID YOU KNOW?

The Dragon Lady wore solid gold shields on her very long fingernails to keep them from breaking.

LEARN MORE! READ THESE ARTICLES...
CLEOPATRA • ELIZABETH I • MAO ZEDONG

Known in the West as the Empress Dowager, Cixi controlled the political life of China for many decades. The nation was fairly stable under her influence, but the government was dishonest and did not make changes that were needed to benefit the people.
© Hulton-Deutsch Collection/Corbis

Answer: Only the servants living within the Forbidden City ever saw the Empress of China.

19

Founder of Pakistan

Mohammed Ali Jinnah was born in Karachi in 1876. At that time the city was part of India, and India was controlled by the British. When Jinnah was a young man, his parents sent him to London to gain business experience. Instead, he studied law and learned about the British system of government. After his studies, he returned to India and began to practice law in Bombay (now Mumbai). It was about this time that the people of India began to seek freedom from British rule.

For hundreds of years, Muslims and Hindus - the area's two major religious groups - had lived together peacefully in India. But there were many more Hindus than Muslims. Because of this, many Muslims feared that they might not be treated equally once India became an independent country.

Mohammed Ali Jinnah.
© Bettmann/Corbis

Although Jinnah was Muslim, at first he didn't think there was anything to be afraid of. But as time passed, he began to feel that the Muslims in India should have their own country. So Jinnah began to work hard to make a Muslim nation out of part of India's land. The new country would be called Pakistan.

In 1947 the British government agreed to the formation of Pakistan. India became independent from Britain in August of that year, and a section of the country became Pakistan. Jinnah was chosen as Pakistan's first head of state, but he served for only a year before he died. Despite his short rule, Jinnah's people loved him. And because he helped create Pakistan, Jinnah is considered the Father of Pakistan.

SEARCH LIGHT

For which people did Jinnah want to build a country?

LEARN MORE! READ THESE ARTICLES...
ASHOKA • MAHATMA GANDHI • NELSON MANDELA

Mohammed Ali Jinnah founded the state of Pakistan in 1947. Here, Pakistani soldiers in 1993 hang a portrait of Jinnah as part of preparations for Pakistan Day in March.
© Reuters NewMedia Inc./Corbis

Answer: Jinnah wanted to build a country for Muslims.

DID YOU KNOW?
In 1993 Nelson Mandela and F.W. de Klerk were jointly awarded the Nobel Prize for Peace for ending the apartheid system.

A Fighter for Rights

South African leader Nelson Mandela was a fighter. He fought against apartheid. Apartheid was an official policy of the government of South Africa that separated people according to their race and colour.

True or false? Mandela spent his life in prison.

During World War II, Mandela joined the African National Congress (ANC), and he later became one of its leaders. This organization had one aim - to fight for the freedom of the black people in South Africa.

Mandela didn't want to use violence in the ANC's fight against the government. However, after the police killed unarmed Africans, Mandela changed his mind. He argued for using **sabotage** against the government - that is, secretly working to undermine and destroy it. At the same time, the South African government outlawed the ANC. In 1962 the government decided that Mandela was guilty of acts against the government. He was sentenced to five years in prison. The following year, he was found guilty of more charges and sentenced to life imprisonment.

Nelson Mandela in 1990.
© David Turnley/Corbis

By the 1980s, more and more people had heard about Mandela's hopes for South Africa. They began to **campaign** for his release from prison. Countries and organizations all over the world gave him their support. Early in 1990, South Africa's president, F.W. de Klerk, ordered Mandela's release. President de Klerk, together with Mandela, worked to change South Africa into a country where all races would have equal rights.

South Africa held its first elections open to people of all races in 1994. Mandela and the ANC won the elections, and Mandela became the country's first black president.

LEARN MORE! READ THESE ARTICLES...
FIDEL CASTRO • MAHATMA GANDHI • MARTIN LUTHER KING JR

Nelson Mandela spent nearly 30 years of his life as a political prisoner. Four years after his release he ran for president of South Africa. He was elected in April 1994.
© Peter Turnley/Corbis

Answer: FALSE. He served a large part of his life - almost 30 years.

Architect of Modern China

Mao Zedong was born in 1893 in China's Hunan province. Mao's father had been born a poor peasant, but he became wealthy as a farmer and grain dealer. Only limited education was available where Mao grew up. So, at the age of 13, he left school to work on his family's farm. He later ran away to attend school in the provincial capital, where he discovered new ideas from Chinese and Western thinkers.

Mao Zedong in 1967.
© Bettmann/Corbis

Mao briefly served in the army during the Chinese Revolution (1911-12). This uprising overthrew the ruling Manchu **dynasty** and turned China into a **republic**. After that there were many years of fighting between different groups who wanted to rule China. This time was known as the 'warlord period'.

After the war, Mao returned to school, ending up at Beijing University, where he worked in the library. There he became involved in the May Fourth Movement of 1919. This was the beginning of China's move towards communism. In communism, property is owned by the state or community, and all citizens are supposed to have a share in the nation's wealth.

In the 1920s, Mao helped create the Chinese Communist Party (CCP). He started a communist revolution among peasants in the countryside. The CCP broke away from the Nationalist Party. The Nationalists thought that the Chinese should decide their own future, but they opposed communism. The Red Army, Mao's military force, began fighting them and gathering strength in the late 1920s.

Mao finally took control of the whole country in 1949 and became the chairman of the People's Republic of China. Although the lives of many poor people were improved under Mao, many others suffered and died during his efforts at reform and improvement. He died on September 9, 1976.

LEARN MORE! READ THESE ARTICLES...
FIDEL CASTRO • CHARLEMAGNE • MOHAMMED ALI JINNAH

SEARCH LIGHT

Was Mao's family rich or poor?

Mao Zedong, the leader of the Chinese communists, spent a great deal of time in the countryside trying to gain support for his ideas. Here, as a young man, he speaks to a group of his followers.
© Bettmann/Corbis

Answer: Actually, they were both. His father was born poor but later became a wealthy farmer and merchant.

Israel's First Woman Prime Minister

In 1906, when Goldie Mabovitch was a child, poverty forced her family to move from Russia to the United States to find work. At school, she

Israeli Prime Minister Golda Meir in 1972.
© Hulton-Deutsch Collection/Corbis

joined a group that wanted Jews to have their own country. This was known as Zionism. A few years later she and her husband, Morris Myerson, moved to Palestine, a Middle Eastern region then under British control.

Goldie Myerson became involved in political activities in Palestine. She **negotiated** protection for Jews who fled from Nazi Europe during World War II. After the war, she worked to help Jewish war refugees.

In 1948 part of Palestine became the State of Israel, and Goldie Myerson was one of the signers of Israel's declaration of independence. The surrounding Arab countries attacked Israel, but the new country defended itself and remained independent.

The following year she was elected to the Knesset, the Israeli **parliament**. Later she changed her last name from Myerson to 'Meir', a Hebrew word meaning 'to burn brightly'. She also became known as 'Golda' instead of Goldie.

Meir became the prime minister of Israel in February 1969. As prime minister, she worked hard for peace in the Middle East and travelled widely to meet with the leaders of many other countries.

But in 1973 Egypt and Syria's invasion of Israel led to another Arab-Israeli war. Though Israel eventually won the war, the whole country was stunned by the attack. Many Israelis felt Meir's government was to blame, and so she resigned as prime minister the following year.

LEARN MORE! READ THESE ARTICLES...
CLEOPATRA • ELIZABETH I • ANWAR EL-SADAT

DID YOU KNOW?
Golda Meir was 71 years old when she became the world's third female prime minister. The first two were Sirimavo R.D. Bandaranaike of Ceylon (now Sri Lanka) and Indira Gandhi of India.

Before she became Israel's prime minister, Golda Meir served as Israel's representative to the United Nations. In this photo, Meir helps a little girl light five candles to celebrate Israel's fifth anniversary.
© Bettmann/Corbis

Answer: Knesset, Palestine, Israel

True or false? Sadat did not want Egypt to be run by a king.

Egypt's Man of Peace

When Muhammad Anwar el-Sadat was born in 1918, Egypt was still a British colony and was ruled by a sultan. But one day Sadat would rise to become Egypt's president.

Sadat was in the army during World War II. After that he joined an organization that wanted to overthrow the Egyptian **monarchy** and drive out the British. The organization was led by Gamal Abdel Nasser. In 1952 Nasser's group was successful, and Egypt gained its independence. Nasser became the country's first president, and Sadat twice served as his vice-president. When Nasser died in 1970, Sadat became president.

Anwar el-Sadat, reviewing a military parade, shortly before he was killed.
© Kevin Fleming/Corbis

Egypt had lost control of the land lying between Egypt and Israel during a war with Israel in 1967. The two countries remained enemies after that. In six years Sadat ordered Egyptian forces to retake this land. Israel won the war that followed. But Sadat's actions made him very popular in Egypt and in other Arab countries.

Four years after the war, Sadat sought peace with Israel. He visited there to share his peace plan. Later he held peace talks in the United States with the Israeli prime minister, Menachem Begin. Because of their efforts, Sadat and Begin shared the 1978 Nobel Prize for Peace.

The following year, Egypt and Israel signed a peace treaty - Israel's first with an Arab country. Sadat's actions were praised around the world. But many Egyptians and other Arabs opposed the treaty. In 1981 Sadat was killed by religious **extremists** during a military parade.

LEARN MORE! READ THESE ARTICLES...
CLEOPATRA • MOHAMMED ALI JINNAH
GOLDA MEIR

DID YOU KNOW?
While Sadat was working to overthrow the Egyptian monarchy, he went to prison twice. The second time he was imprisoned, he taught himself French and English.

When Egypt and Israel were working to make peace, U.S. President Jimmy Carter was a great help. Here (from left to right) you see Sadat's wife, Jehan, and Sadat himself, with the U.S. first lady, Rosalynn Carter, and President Carter.
© Wally McNamee/Corbis

Answer: TRUE.

World Peacemaker

A peacemaker has to be impartial - that is, be fair and not take sides. U Thant was a true peacemaker. As the secretary-general of the United Nations between 1961 and 1971, he had the job of peacemaker among many warring countries.

U Thant was born in 1909 in Burma (now called Myanmar). 'U' is not a name but a term of respect similar to the English word 'Mister'. Thant means 'pure'. Thant was educated at the University of Rangoon. It was here that he met Thakin Nu, later called U Nu. U Nu went on to become the prime minister of Burma after World War II.

Nu recognized Thant's abilities and appointed him as a spokesman for the government. Later Thant became a **diplomat** when he was appointed a member of the Burmese representatives to the United Nations (UN). In 1957 he became his country's permanent representative to the UN, and he later served as vice president of the UN General Assembly.

When the UN's leader, the secretary-general, died in 1961, the United States and the Soviet Union could not agree on a new leader for the body. Though neither country got their first choice, they were able to settle on Thant as acceptable.

As secretary-general, Thant worked for peace around the world. In 1962 he aided in the removal of Soviet missiles from Cuba. He also helped to end the civil war in the Congo, and he established a peacekeeping force on Cyprus in the Mediterranean Sea. When India and Pakistan went to war in 1965, Thant flew to India to help negotiate the ceasefire.

LEARN MORE! READ THESE ARTICLES...
MAHATMA GANDHI • MARTIN LUTHER KING JR
NELSON MANDELA

SEARCH LIGHT

True or false? U is U Thant's first name.

DID YOU KNOW?

In 1976 an island in New York's East River, near the UN headquarters, was decorated with trees and flowers and called U Thant.

U Thant was a faithful Buddhist, and he applied a Buddhist attitude of focus and open-mindedness to his work at the United Nations.

© Bettmann/Corbis

Answer: FALSE. U has a meaning similar to the word 'Mister'.

DID YOU KNOW?

A new English translation of Anne Frank's diary was published in 1995. The new edition has material that was not in the original version and is nearly one-third longer.

SEARCH LIGHT

True or false? Anne Frank went on to write many other famous books.

A Young Girl and Her Diary

Anne Frank.
Anne Frank House, Amsterdam and Anne Frank-Fonds,
Basel—Hulton/Archive by Getty Images

During World War II in Europe, the Nazis of Germany tried to destroy the Jewish people and their culture. The Nazis had taken control of many countries, including the Netherlands (Holland). In the city of Amsterdam, the Nazi threat forced a young Jewish girl and her family to spend two years in hiding. Anne Frank's moving diary of those years in hiding has since become a classic book.

Halfway through the war, the Nazis began sending Jews to prison camps. So in July 1942, Anne's family went into hiding in the back-room office and warehouse of Anne's father's business. Four other Jews hid with them in the small space, and non-Jewish friends smuggled food and other supplies to them.

Anne was 13 when she went into hiding. In her diary, she describes daily life in the secret rooms. She also writes about her own dreams and feelings while growing up in hiding.

The family never once left their hideout until the Nazi police discovered them in August 1944. Then the Frank family was moved to the concentration camp at Auschwitz in Poland, where Anne's mother died in 1945. Anne and her sister were sent to another camp, Bergen-Belsen, where they both died of typhus. Anne's father, Otto Frank, was the only family member who survived.

Friends had found Anne's diary in the hiding space. After the war, they gave it to her father, and he published it in 1947. Since then, Anne's story of courage and hope has inspired millions of readers. Today, the Frank family's hiding place in Amsterdam is a museum.

LEARN MORE! READ THESE ARTICLES...
MAHATMA GANDHI • HELEN KELLER • MARTIN LUTHER KING JR

Anne Frank sits at her desk at school in 1940.
She left school at the age of 13 to go into hiding.
Anne Frank House, Amsterdam and Anne Frank-Fonds,
Basel—Hulton/Archive by Getty Images

Answer: FALSE. Anne died during World War II, and her diary is the only writing of hers that survived.

DID YOU KNOW?
The money in Venezuela is named for the South American liberator Simón Bolívar. It's called the *bolívar*.

Hero of Many Nations

In the early 1800s, in the country that would become Venezuela, there lived a man with a big dream. He wanted the countries of Spanish South America to become independent from Spain and join together as one strong country.

This man was Simón Bolívar. For years he fought the Spanish in support of this dream, and many people came to help him from all over the world. Many of them sailed from Europe and searched all over South America to find him.

Bolívar was born in 1783. His **liberation** of New Granada - now Colombia, Ecuador, and parts of several other countries - is one of the most daring acts in the history of war. In the spring of 1819 he led a small army of 2,500 men through floodwaters and

True or false? Bolívar made all of South America come together as one nation.

Portrait of Simón Bolívar by M.N. Bate.
© Bettmann/Corbis

across icy mountain passes, through places where there were no paths at all. Tired and hungry, they finally arrived in Boyacá, near Bogotá, the capital of New Granada. There they surprised a big Spanish army. Fighting fiercely, they beat the Spanish and freed New Granada.

Bolívar fought many battles to free other countries in South America, including his native Venezuela. His dream of freeing the South American countries from Spain came true. But even if he was never able to join all the different countries together as one nation, he is one of the most important heroes in South America. The South American country of Bolivia was named in his honour.

LEARN MORE! READ THESE ARTICLES…
JULIUS CAESAR • FIDEL CASTRO • CHARLEMAGNE

In addition to the countries that are now Colombia and Ecuador, Simón Bolívar and his troops won the independence of Venezuela and Peru.
© Bettmann/Corbis

Answer: FALSE. He did, however, help free many nations from Spanish rule.

35

Salt and Empires

In March of 1930, a 61-year-old Indian man started out on a long walk to the ocean. When people asked where he was going, Mohandas ('Mahatma') Gandhi replied, 'I am going to the ocean to get some salt.' Soon thousands joined him in a trip that lasted a month and became known as the 'Salt March'.

Mohandas K. Gandhi was a Hindu Indian who had studied law in London. India was controlled by Britain, and when Gandhi returned home he was angered by the poverty and inequality he saw in his country. Rather than fight the British with guns or bombs, Gandhi believed in simply refusing to obey unjust laws. For example, he urged Indians to make their own clothing so they wouldn't have to buy British goods. Hindus began to call Gandhi 'Mahatma', which means 'great soul'.

Mahatma Gandhi.
© Bettmann/Corbis

> **DID YOU KNOW?**
> In the Hindi language, Gandhi's principle of non-violence is known as satyagraha. The word means 'truth force'.

Most Indians could not afford to buy expensive British salt, but it was against the law for them to make their own. So Gandhi walked 300 kilometres to the sea to make salt from seawater. After the Salt March, the British put Gandhi in jail. It wasn't the first or the last time he was jailed for leading non-violent protests. Gandhi went to jail cheerfully. When he came out, he went back to teaching Indians how to regain control of their country by peaceful means. India finally won independence from Britain in 1947.

After India became independent, there was violence between the country's Hindu and Muslim populations. During the last year of his life, Gandhi worked to build peace between all the peoples of India.

LEARN MORE! READ THESE ARTICLES...
MOHAMMED ALI JINNAH • MARTIN LUTHER KING JR • MOTHER TERESA

Mahatma Gandhi, leader of the Indian non-violent protest, marches with supporters to the shore at Dandi to collect salt in violation of the law. Following this action, he was jailed.
© Bettmann/Corbis

Answer: FALSE. Mohandas was his name. Mahatma was a title of respect.

Civil Rights Leader

On 1 December 1955, in Montgomery, Alabama, U.S., a black woman called Rosa Parks was arrested. She had refused to give up her seat on a bus to a white man. At that time, the law said that black people had to sit only in certain sections of trains and buses

Martin Luther King Jr riding a bus in Montgomery, Alabama, U.S., in 1956.
© Bettmann/Corbis

and use different public toilets and even drinking fountains from the ones white people used. Rosa Parks's action sparked protests by black residents of the city. And Martin Luther King Jr was chosen to lead the protests.

True or false? Martin Luther King Jr set off the Montgomery bus boycott.

King was a Baptist minister and a student of the Indian leader Mahatma Gandhi. He believed that non-violence was the most powerful way for people to make their point. This means demanding rights through peaceful methods, such as **strikes** and protests, not by fighting. The protests he led became known as the Montgomery bus **boycott**. The law was changed after a year of protests.

However, black people still didn't receive the same rights and privileges as white people. In 1963 King and his supporters were imprisoned because of their protests against **discrimination**. When he was freed, King and other **civil rights** leaders organized a march on Washington, D.C., the national capital. There, King delivered a powerful speech to hundreds of thousands of people, saying: 'I have a dream.' His dream was that one day all people would be equal, like brothers.

For his work on civil rights, King was awarded the Nobel Prize for Peace in 1964. Through all his struggles, King used only peaceful methods of protest. But in April 1968, King was shot dead in Memphis, Tennessee, by James Earl Ray.

LEARN MORE! READ THESE ARTICLES…
MAHATMA GANDHI • NELSON MANDELA • MOTHER TERESA

Martin Luther King Jr led the march on Washington in 1963. His protests helped win important rights for African Americans.

DID YOU KNOW?
In 1977, King was posthumously (after his death) awarded the Presidential Medal of Freedom. This is the U.S. government's highest honour awarded to a person not in the military.

Answer: FALSE. Rosa Parks set off the boycott when she refused to give up her seat.

Around-the-World Voyager

Hundreds of years ago, only very brave men took the risk of travelling the open seas to reach unknown lands. Ferdinand Magellan was one such man.

Magellan was born into a **noble** family in Portugal in about 1480. When he was about 25, he joined the Portuguese navy, where he fought in numerous battles and saw many new places. But the king of Portugal refused to increase his **wages** after a decade of service, so Magellan went to work for the Spanish king.

An illustration of Ferdinand Magellan's ship Victoria.
Collection of the Bibliotheque Nationale; photo, © Erich Lessing/Art Resource, New York

At that time, Portugal controlled the sea route around Africa to the Indian Ocean to reach the rich Spice Islands (now called the East Indies). Magellan decided to sail west to find a new route to the islands. He set out in 1519, sailing across the Atlantic and down the coast of South America. He hoped to discover a passage to the ocean beyond South America. When he found it, he named it the Strait of Magellan. The ocean on the other side appeared calm and peaceful. Magellan called it the Pacific, from the Latin word for 'peaceful'.

After 99 more days, Magellan's ship reached the island now known as Guam. Landing in the islands we call the Philippines, Magellan and his men fought with islanders. Magellan was killed there on 27 April 1521.

A crewman, Juan Sebastián de Elcano, took command. The remaining crew sailed to the Spice Islands, loaded up with spices, and returned to Spain. In a voyage that took more than three years, they became the first men to circle the globe. But during that time, 200 men had died.

LEARN MORE! READ THESE ARTICLES…
SIMÓN BOLÍVAR • GALILEO GALILEI • TENZING NORGAY

SEARCH LIGHT

Unscramble the following words:
- utgroPal
- ciSpe sladIns
- fiPicac nOace

This painting from 1970 shows the Portuguese explorer Ferdinand Magellan. He led an expedition that was first to travel all the way around the Earth.
The Art Archive/Marine Museum, Lisbon/Dagli Orti

Answer: utgroPal = **Portugal**
ciSpe sladIns = **Spice Islands**
fiPicac nOace = **Pacific Ocean**

On Top of the World

On 29 May 1953, at 11.30 AM, Tenzing Norgay and Edmund Hillary became the first people to reach the **summit** of the highest mountain on Earth, Mount Everest.

Tenzing Norgay was born in 1914 in Tibet (now part of China). He later moved to Nepal and lived with the Sherpa people. Sherpas, who moved from Tibet to Nepal hundreds of years ago, have lived in high mountains for hundreds of years.

Tenzing Norgay.
UPI—EB Inc.

Not far from Tenzing's adopted village rises the majestic Everest. It is part of the Himalaya Mountains and lies on the border between Nepal and Tibet. When Europeans went to Nepal to climb mountains, many Sherpas were hired to carry supplies for the mountain climbers. Because of their experience living in high mountains, they proved to be excellent guides and **mountaineers**.

At the age of 18, Tenzing moved to Darjeeling (Darjiling), in India. He hoped to earn his living carrying supplies for mountaineering expeditions. Three years later, he accompanied a survey team as a **porter** on an expedition to climb Mount Everest. During the next few years, he took part in more Everest expeditions than any other climber.

Working with so many different people, Tenzing learned to speak seven languages. Later he became a *sirdar*, or an organizer of porters. He continued to guide expeditions to Everest and inspired many mountaineers.

During their historic climb of Mount Everest in 1953, Edmund Hillary lost his footing and nearly died. Tenzing did not panic. He held the rope line tightly and planted his axe firmly in the ice. Later he simply said, 'Mountain climbers always help one another.'

For his courage and heroism and for having been one of the first people to scale Mount Everest, Tenzing was awarded the British George Cross and the Star of Nepal.

LEARN MORE! READ THESE ARTICLES...
ASHOKA • GALILEO GALILEI • FERDINAND MAGELLAN

DID YOU KNOW?
Tenzing Norgay was the first man to be photographed on the summit of Everest. Since Tenzing could not operate a camera, Edmund Hillary took the photograph.

Here, Edmund Hillary (on the left) and Tenzing Norgay prepare for one part of their climb to the top of Mount Everest.
Royal Geographical Society; photo, Alfred Gregory

SEARCH LIGHT

Fill in the gap: Someone who organizes porters for mountain climbing in the Himalayas is called a _____.

Answer: Someone who organizes porters for mountain climbing in the Himalayas is called a *sirdar*.

Mother
of the Poor and Dying

During her lifetime Mother Teresa became known worldwide for her kindness and her **charitable** work.

Mother Teresa was born Agnes Gonxha Bojaxhiu in Albania (now Macedonia) in 1910. When she was 18 years old, she decided to become a nun in the Roman Catholic church. She travelled to Ireland and there she joined the Institute of the Blessed Virgin Mary. She took **vows** promising to live a simple life and not to marry, and she became Sister Teresa.

The Institute had charity missions in India, and soon Sister Teresa sailed to the country to work as a teacher. Over the next 17 years, she taught in two schools in India, one of which was in Calcutta (now Kolkata). She saw firsthand the poverty and suffering of the people. She often said that she was inspired to make two important decisions in her life. One was to become a nun, and in 1946 the other was to devote her life to helping the sick and the poor.

As soon as her studies in nursing were finished, she began working with the people living in Calcutta's slums. She became an Indian citizen. And she became Mother Teresa when she founded the Missionaries of Charity. This was a new order of Roman Catholic nuns who wanted to help the sick, especially the dying and disabled.

Under Mother Teresa's guidance, the Missionaries of Charity opened centres all over the world. In these centres anyone could receive care, no matter what their religion. In 1979 Mother Teresa was awarded the Nobel Prize for Peace. Soon after her death, in 1997, the Roman Catholic church began the process to have Mother Teresa declared a saint.

LEARN MORE! READ THESE ARTICLES...
ELIZABETH BLACKWELL • MAHATMA GANDHI
JANE GOODALL

SEARCH LIGHT

Was
Mother Teresa
Indian
by birth?

Mother Teresa lived in poverty with some of India's poorest people. She made it her life's work to care for the country's poor and dying.
© Bettmann/Corbis

DID YOU KNOW?
When Mother Teresa founded her religious order, the Missionaries of Charity, her Indian nuns adopted the *sari* as their habit, or official dress. The *sari* is a garment worn by most women of India, Pakistan, and Bangladesh.

Answer: No. Mother Teresa was born in Albania (now Macedonia), near Greece. But she lived and worked in India and became an Indian citizen.

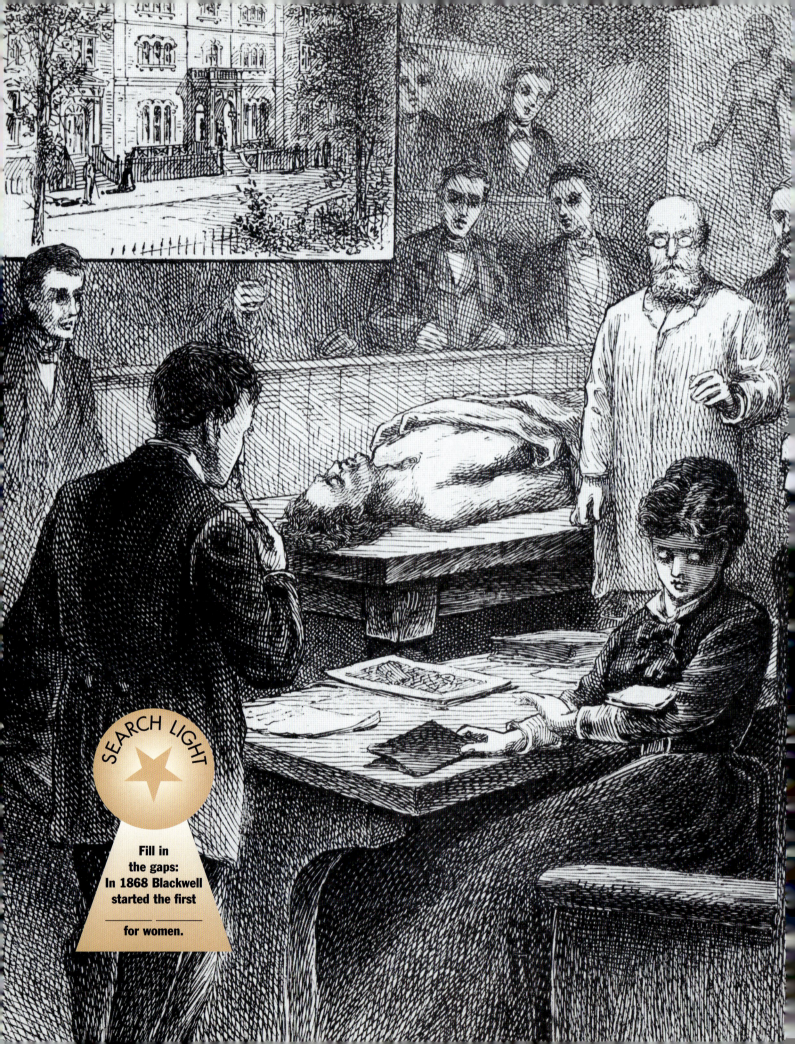

The First Modern Woman Doctor

Elizabeth Blackwell was born in England in 1821, but she moved to the United States with her family when she was 11. By the time she was 23, Blackwell had decided that she wanted to be a doctor. But at this time there were no female doctors in the United States.

It wasn't easy for Blackwell to study medicine. Most of the medical colleges she applied to turned her down. The men who taught medicine didn't think it was right for a woman to be a doctor. Finally Blackwell was admitted to Geneva Medical College in New York. She was the only woman in a class of 150.

The other medical students made things difficult for Blackwell. They criticized her, refused to talk to her, and kept her from taking part in the classroom medical demonstrations. However, two years later Blackwell was the best student in her class. In 1849 she became the first female doctor in the United States.

Despite this training, Blackwell could not get a job in any of the city hospitals. So she opened her own hospital, the New York Infirmary for Women and Children, in a district where many poor people lived. When the American Civil War broke out in 1861, Blackwell's hospital became a relief centre for wounded soldiers. She also helped select and train nurses for the war.

Blackwell worked to establish a medical school for women, so that other women could become doctors. In 1868 she opened the Woman's Medical College, the first of its kind in America.

DID YOU KNOW?
A year after Blackwell opened her hospital, her sister Emily came to work with her. She, too, had become a doctor.

Photograph of Elizabeth Blackwell.
Courtesy, Hobart and William Smith Colleges

LEARN MORE! READ THESE ARTICLES...
JANE GOODALL • LOUIS PASTEUR • MOTHER TERESA

Elizabeth Blackwell was not only the first American woman doctor. She also became the first woman to have her name placed on the British medical register. This meant she was allowed to practice medicine in Great Britain.
© Bettmann/Corbis

Answer: In 1868 Blackwell started the first medical school (or medical college) for women.

47

Gold Medallist in Athletics

SEARCH LIGHT

How many Olympic Games has Freeman competed in?
a) 1
b) 2
c) 3

When she won the 400-metre world championship in 1997, Cathy Freeman ran a victory lap carrying two flags. One was the flag of her country, Australia. The other was that of her people, the Aboriginals. The Aboriginals are the original people of Australia, who have suffered great mistreatment and injustice since the Europeans came to their country. Her choice to carry both flags was **controversial**. But it showed Freeman's strong sense of national and ethnic pride.

Cathy Freeman holding the Olympic torch in 2000.
© Reuters NewMedia Inc./Corbis

While Freeman was growing up in Queensland, her father encouraged her to start running. By the time she was 17, Freeman had won a gold medal at the 1990 Commonwealth Games and been named Young Australian of the Year. In 1992 she was the first Australian Aboriginal woman to compete in the Olympic Games.

At the 1994 Commonwealth Games, Freeman took home gold medals in the 400-metre and 200-metre races. Her win in the 200-metre race set a national record. Perhaps Freeman's greatest race was at the 1996 Olympic Games in Atlanta, Georgia, U.S. She ran against the world record holder, Marie-José Pérec of France. The two champions raced neck and neck. Finally, it was Pérec who shot ahead to the finish line.

In 1997 Freeman was named Australian of the Year. A year later, however, she injured her foot and had to withdraw from the Commonwealth Games. Freeman didn't let the injury stop her, and in 1999 she was running again. She came back and successfully defended her 400-metre world championship title. At the Sydney Olympics in 2000, Freeman had the great honour of lighting the Olympic torch. A week later her dream of Olympic gold came true when she won the 400-metre race in front of her fellow Australians. Again she took her victory lap proudly carrying both the Australian and Aboriginal flags.

LEARN MORE! READ THESE ARTICLES...
HELEN KELLER • PELÉ • TENZING NORGAY

Cathy Freeman was the first Aboriginal to win an individual medal in an Olympic event. She won the 400-metre race at the 2000 Olympics in Sydney, Australia.
© Duomo/Corbis

DID YOU KNOW?
In a rush to get to her first track race, 8-year-old Cathy Freeman ran into a post and hurt her eye. She ran her first race with one eye closed and won it easily.

This fresco (a painting created on wet plaster) shows
Galileo demonstrating his version of the telescope.
© Archivo Iconografico, S.A./Corbis

The Man Who Discovered Outer Space

Galileo Galilei was born in Pisa, Italy, in 1564. As a young man he became interested in mathematics and **astronomy**. He loved to experiment and try out new ideas.

A story claims that Galileo once dropped objects of different weights from the top of the famous Leaning Tower of Pisa. He wanted to prove that things fall at the same speed, no matter how much they weigh. But some of Galileo's ideas angered other scientists, so he left Pisa and went to Padua.

Galileo.
© Bettmann/Corbis

For years Galileo taught mathematics at the University of Padua. But in 1609 his career changed direction. Galileo heard about the telescope, a Dutch invention that could make distant objects appear closer. Galileo figured out how such a device would work and then used **lenses** from spectacle makers' shops to make his own telescopes. Galileo's telescopes were better than most and could make objects appear up to 20 times larger than what the naked eye could see.

Galileo began to look up into the night sky. In December 1609, with the help of his telescope, Galileo learned that the Moon's surface is rough and uneven. A month later he discovered four moons orbiting the planet Jupiter. Also, when Galileo studied Saturn, he noticed something mysterious about its appearance. Later scientists would learn that the planet's strange look was due to its large rings.

Using his telescopes, Galileo helped change how people looked up at space. Likewise, much of the modern science of **physics** is based on his ideas - especially his ideas about how objects of all sizes move and how helpful it is to test scientific ideas by experimenting.

LEARN MORE! READ THESE ARTICLES...
ELIZABETH BLACKWELL • FERDINAND MAGELLAN
LOUIS PASTEUR

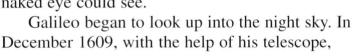

SEARCH LIGHT

Fill in the gap: Galileo built his own _____, which was an improvement on others built earlier.

The Woman Who Lived with Chimpanzees

In the 1940s a young English girl named Jane Goodall dreamed of living in the African forests among the animals she'd read about. As she grew older, Goodall began to make her dream come true.

Jane Goodall presenting a stuffed toy monkey to United Nations Secretary-General Kofi Annan in 2002.
© AFP/Corbis

In 1957, when she was about 23 years old, a school friend invited Goodall to Kenya, in Africa. While in Africa, Goodall met the famous scientist Dr Louis Leakey. At the time, Leakey was studying wild chimpanzees in order to find out more about the origins of human life. He was impressed by Goodall's interest in animals and encouraged her to study chimpanzees in Tanzania.

Some people thought that Goodall wouldn't last for more than a few months in the forest amongst the wild animals. But Goodall proved them wrong and ended up living in Tanzania for 15 years. During that time, the chimpanzees slowly became used to Goodall and finally allowed her to spend hours around them.

Being able to watch the chimpanzees up close allowed Goodall to discover many things about the animals that people did not know. Goodall saw chimpanzees use sticks as simple tools to draw termites and ants out of their nests. Goodall also found that all chimpanzees are different from each other in their behaviour and **natures**, just like people.

As a child, Jane Goodall grew up reading about wild animals. But as an adult, she ended up writing many books of her own. In them she shared what she learned from 15 years of living with the wild chimpanzees of Africa.

LEARN MORE! READ THESE ARTICLES...
ELIZABETH BLACKWELL • LOUIS PASTEUR
TENZING NORGAY

DID YOU KNOW?

Before Goodall's studies, scientists believed chimpanzees were vegetarians. But Goodall learned that they do sometimes hunt and eat meat.

Jane Goodall spent many years in Africa studying chimpanzees. She encountered this curious chimp at the Gombe Stream Research Center in Tanzania in 1972.
© Bettmann/Corbis

SEARCH LIGHT

Jane Goodall liked to read about Tarzan, Mowgli, and Dr Dolittle. What do all three storybook characters have in common?

Answer: Tarzan, Mowgli, and Dr Dolittle all lived with animals.

Helen Keller (on the left) is shown here reading the lips of her teacher, Anne Sullivan (on the right). Sullivan stayed with her pupil from 1887 until her own death in 1936.
© Corbis

Woman of Courage

Helen Keller became blind and deaf soon after she was born, but she still managed to learn to read, write, and speak.

Helen was born in Alabama in the United States in 1880. At 19 months old she fell ill, probably with scarlet fever. She recovered but lost her

Helen Keller in her later years.
EB Inc.

eyesight and hearing. Since she couldn't hear other people, she didn't learn to speak.

When Helen was 6 years old, Alexander Graham Bell examined her. He was a doctor for speech correction as well as being the inventor of the telephone. Bell sent a special teacher, Anne Sullivan, to stay with Helen as her **governess**.

Sullivan was herself a remarkable woman. She was very patient and taught Helen that things had names. She taught Helen to finger spell the alphabet. By using finger spelling on Helen's palm, Sullivan helped Helen understand names for things that she could feel.

Helen was a hard worker and soon learned to read a form of the alphabet with her fingers. She started to read by feeling raised letters and words on cardboard. Later she learned **Braille**, a system of writing that many blind people use. Another teacher, Sarah Fuller, taught Helen to speak by having her feel people's lips and throats as they were talking.

Despite her blindness, Helen Keller wrote numerous articles and several books, including *The Story of My Life* and *Helen Keller's Journal*. Her early life with Anne Sullivan is the subject of a well-known play and film called *The Miracle Worker*.

Helen Keller died when she was 88 years old. She is remembered as a woman of great courage and intelligence.

LEARN MORE! READ THESE ARTICLES...
ELIZABETH BLACKWELL • ANNE FRANK
CATHY FREEMAN

DID YOU KNOW?
As an adult, Helen Keller lectured all over the world. And her efforts to improve the treatment of deaf and blind people helped to stop the practice of putting people with physical disabilities into asylums for the mentally ill.

Answer: FALSE. Helen Keller became deaf and blind after an illness when she was almost 2 years old.

DID YOU KNOW?

In 1868 Pasteur saved the French silk industry. Silk businesses were facing ruin because of a mysterious disease that attacked the silkworms. Pasteur worked out a way of detecting the disease and preventing it from spreading.

The Man Who Conquered Disease

In the 1800s, the bite of a dog with rabies meant certain death for the person who had been bitten. In 1885, when a rabid dog bit a boy called Joseph Meister, his mother was desperate. She went to the only man she thought might be able to cure her son.

Pasteur had found that rabies was caused by a virus - a disease-causing **agent** so small it could not be seen, even under a microscope. He had already worked out a way to defeat the rabies virus in animals. But he had never tried his treatment on humans. Pasteur treated Joseph, and Joseph became the first person to be cured of rabies.

Pasteur devoted his life to solving the problems of industry, farming, and medicine. He discovered that if a liquid like milk is heated to a certain temperature for a few minutes, it takes longer to spoil. If milk is not treated in this way, tiny living organisms called 'bacteria' cause it to go bad. These organisms are killed by heat in a process that came to be called 'pasteurization'.

Pasteur also discovered that many diseases are caused by germs that enter the body from outside. In 1877 he tried to find a cure for anthrax, a disease that affects the lungs and kills cattle and sheep. Pasteur successfully developed the method known as 'immunization'. Immunization means giving a patient a weak dose of a virus that the patient can fight off. Then the patient's body knows how to stop an actual case of the disease.

SEARCH LIGHT

Pasteurization refers to
a) a disease-causing organism.
b) a weak dose of a disease.
c) heating something to kill bacteria.

Scientist Louis Pasteur.
© Hulton-Deutsch Collection/Corbis

LEARN MORE! READ THESE ARTICLES...
ELIZABETH BLACKWELL • GALILEO GALILEI • MOTHER TERESA

Louis Pasteur's discoveries are among the most important in the history of medical science. He is often known as the founder of microbiology - the study of simple life forms too small to be seen with the naked eye.
© Hulton-Deutsch Collection/Corbis

Football Star

One man, more than any other, has helped to make football (soccer) popular around the world. That man is Pelé. Pelé, whose real name is Edson Arantes do Nascimento, was born in 1940 in Brazil.

Pelé made his **debut** with the Santos Football Club in 1956. With Pelé playing forward, the team won several South American cups. In 1962 the team won its first world championship. Pelé also played for Brazil's national team and helped it to win the World Cup championship in 1958, 1962, and 1970.

Pelé holding international football award for 'Footballer of the Century'.
© AFP/Corbis

Pelé was a brilliant player who possessed great speed and balance. He could guess the moves of other players and had good control of the ball. In addition to all this, he could kick a ball powerfully with either foot, or direct it with his head, straight into the goal.

Pelé scored a career total of 1,281 goals in 1,363 matches, with 139 in one year alone. He scored his 1,000th goal in 1969. Pelé's career made him a national hero in Brazil. His fans call him Pérola Negra, meaning 'Black Pearl'.

Although Pelé retired in 1974, he made a comeback the following year with a New York team, the Cosmos. He said he returned to 'make soccer truly popular in the United States.' He succeeded, becoming a star in the United States as well.

Pelé's skills did not stop on the football field. He has also written best-selling **autobiographies**, starred in several films, and composed music, including the whole soundtrack for the 1977 film *Pelé*.

LEARN MORE! READ THESE ARTICLES…
SIMÓN BOLÍVAR • CATHY FREEMAN • TENZING NORGAY

Pelé in action was so magical to watch that once two armies stopped fighting just to watch him play.
© AFP/Corbis

DID YOU KNOW?
When Pelé first went for trials with the major league football teams, he was repeatedly turned down.

Æ tat . suæ . 34 .

DID YOU KNOW?
Shakespeare was so imaginative in his use of language that he created, or 'coined', over 2,000 words or sayings that people have used ever since.

Plays That Never Grow Old

William Shakespeare is considered to be the greatest playwright in the English language and one of the most beloved playwrights in the world.

Not much is known about Shakespeare's life. He was born in Stratford-upon-Avon, England, in 1564. This was during the **reign** of Queen Elizabeth I. In his late 20s, Shakespeare went to the city of London to write and act. He joined a theatre **troupe** and began to write plays.

Over the next 20 years, Shakespeare wrote 38 plays and many poems. From his writing we can tell that he knew a lot about human feelings, as

2001 production of *A Midsummer Night's Dream* performed at the Albery Theatre in London.
© Archivo Iconografico, S.A./Corbis

well as both city and country life. Most of the stories that Shakespeare told were known to his audience. But his characters and the way he told their stories in his plays attracted crowds of people to the Globe Theatre, where his troupe often performed.

Four hundred years later, people still enjoy reading Shakespeare's plays and seeing them onstage and in films. They quote his most famous lines (such as 'To be or not to be') and laugh and cry along with his characters. Shakespeare's plays have remained popular for several reasons. His characters show realistic human emotions. His **plots** are often complicated, but they always hold the audience's attention. And his language is powerful and poetic.

Some of Shakespeare's plays, such as *Hamlet*, have very sad endings. They are called 'tragedies'. Others, such as *A Midsummer Night's Dream*, are full of silly plots and have happy endings. They are the 'comedies'. Other Shakespeare plays, such as *Julius Caesar* or *Henry V*, are based on real-life figures and events. These are the 'histories'. And some plays, such as *Romeo and Juliet,* have a little bit of everything: romance, comedy, *and* tragedy.

LEARN MORE! READ THESE ARTICLES...
JULIUS CAESAR • ELIZABETH I • GOLDA MEIR

William Shakespeare's plays have been popular for hundreds of years. Shown here is a portrait of the famous playwright.
© Robbie Jack/Corbis

SEARCH LIGHT

Which of the following describes a play with a happy ending?
a) tragedy
b) comedy
c) plot

Answer: b) comedy

G L O S S A R Y

agent something that produces an effect

astronomy (adjective: astronomical) the science of the heavenly bodies and of their sizes, motions, and composition

autobiography life story written by the person it is about

bond connection or friendship

boycott the refusal to deal with a person, group, or country, usually in order to show disapproval or to force a change in behaviour

Braille a system of writing for the blind in which letters are represented by raised dots

campaign planned activities designed to lead to a particular result

charitable done to serve the needs of the poor or sick

civil rights the social and personal rights of a citizen

communism (adjective: communist) system of government in which all property is owned by the state or community and all citizens are supposed to have a share in the total wealth

conflict disagreement, struggle, or fighting

controversial causing division or disagreement

debut first formal public appearance

dictator person who rules with total power, often in a cruel or brutal way

diplomat person who works to keep up friendly relations between the governments of different countries

discrimination the treatment of some individuals or groups differently from others without any fair or proper reason

dynasty series of rulers of the same family

edict law or order given by a ruler or leader

extremist person who holds unusually strong opinions or beliefs

governess woman who teaches and trains a child in a private home

guerrilla person who is part of an independent fighting force that makes surprise raids behind enemy lines

immortal living or lasting forever

lens (plural: lenses) curved piece of glass that concentrates rays of light

liberation freedom

monarchy form of government in which the ruler inherits the position and rules for life; monarchs include kings, queens, emperors, and tsars

mountaineer mountain climber

nature inborn or instinctive way of behaving or thinking

negotiate to discuss and bargain with another in order to reach an agreement

noble of upper-class birth or rank

nuclear weapon explosive device that produces enormous power by splitting apart the centres of the tiny particles called "atoms"

parliament the law-making body of some governments

physics the science that deals with matter and energy and the way they interact

plot the main story of a work of literature

pope the leader of the Roman Catholic church

porter person who carries baggage

rebel person who fights against an existing power or way of doing things

reign the time during which a ruler is in power

republic form of government in which citizens are allowed to elect officials and representatives responsible for governing by law

ruthless without pity

sabotage damage or destruction of property that interferes with an enemy's use of it

Soviet Union country of eastern Europe and northern Asia that existed from 1922 to 1991 and consisted of Russia and 14 other republics

strike temporary stopping of normal activities in protest against an act or condition

summit top or highest point

troupe company or group; *especially*, a working group of stage performers

vow solemn promise or statement

wages payment for work or services

I N D E X